FACE THE FATS

Eating the right foods is one of the easiest and most important ways to keep your body healthy. For your body to be the best that it can be, you must eat a well balanced diet. This means a diet that includes the six types of nutrients your body needs. These are water, vitamins, minerals, carbohydrates, fats, and proteins. When you eat well, your body works better. A well balanced diet may contain many different types of food. It might even include some things that you think you're better off without!

Take fat, for example. What do you think of when you hear that a food has fat in it? You might think that the food is not good for you or that it is unhealthy. Yet your diet should have a certain amount of fat in it for your body to stay healthy.

THE IMPORTANCE OF FAT

One of the most important functions of fat is to store energy for the body. Most of this energy is stored in cells called *adipose cells*, also known as *fat cells*. Fats store energy very efficiently. They can store twice as much energy as an equal amount of proteins or carbohydrates.

Fats take longer to digest, so you feel full longer after you eat them. The body uses energy from fat for all its important functions. This energy can help power movement, digestion, and other activities. When energy is needed, fat cells release the stored fat into the bloodstream. Cells that need fuel take in the fat and break it down, releasing the stored energy.

Fats have other important functions, too. They carry vitamins and minerals throughout the body. Vitamins A, D, E, and K are all carried by fats. Fats also help nerve cells and other cells function properly. Layers of fat cells inside the body protect our vital organs and help insulate the body.

THE RIGHT AMOUNT OF FAT

Your body gets fats from the foods you eat. But how much fat is good for you? *Nutritionists,* people who study foods and diets, say that only a small amount of fat is necessary each day. However, small children need more fat. From infancy to age 2, children need fats to give their bodies the energy needed for quick growth. Fats are especially important for nerve and brain tissue growth.

Nuts contain unsaturated fats.

Most Americans don't have to worry about getting too little fat in their diets. Experts say that the average American eats between six and eight times too much fat in his or her daily diet. An excess amount of fat can be a bad thing. People who have too much fat in their diets can suffer from a variety of problems, including *obesity.* Obesity is the condition of having 20 percent or more body fat than is considered healthy. According to one study conducted by the Centers for Disease Control, one out of every three Americans weighs more than he or she should.

People who have too much fat in their diets may also have high levels of *cholesterol* in their blood. Cholesterol is a waxy substance that is found naturally in almost all human tissue. A certain amount of cholesterol is good for you. But too much cholesterol can build up in the blood vessels, slowing the flow of blood through the body. Cholesterol buildup can lead to such serious problems as heart attacks and strokes. Heart disease is the number one cause of death among adults in the United States.

How much fat is the right amount for you? The American Heart Association (AHA) recommends that fats account for no more than 30 percent of a person's total daily *calories.* Calories are the units nutritionists use to measure the amounts of energy supplied by different foods. If you consume 2,400 calories a day, 800 or fewer should come from fat.

Fats have about twice as many calories per gram as other dietary nutrients such as carbohydrates or proteins. Each gram of fat has 9 calories. Each gram of protein or carbohydrate has 4 calories. Excess calories that the body does not need right away are stored as body fat. Fats are more responsible for obesity problems than sugars and starches are. Most nutritionists recommend reducing the amounts of all fats in the diet.

GOOD FAT, BAD FAT

Low-fat or skim milk is a healthy choice.

There are three important kinds of fats. They are *saturated, monounsaturated,* and *polyunsaturated.* Most foods have all three types of fats in different amounts. Some foods have more saturated fats. Others have more unsaturated fats.

High levels of saturated fats are found in red meat and in dairy products such as cheese and butter. They are usually solid at room temperature. Other foods that contain saturated fats include eggs, whole milk, ice cream, coconut and palm oil, and chocolate. Saturated fats are considered "bad" fats. They can increase the level of cholesterol in the blood. Most nutritionists recommend reducing the amount of saturated fats you consume. Of the 30 percent of total daily calories from fat, the AHA recommends that only 10 percent come from saturated fats.

Saturated fats come chiefly from animal sources. High levels of unsaturated fats are found in fish, nuts, and vegetable oils. Monounsaturated and polyunsaturated fats are both liquids at room temperature. Monounsaturated fats can be found in such vegetable oils as olive, canola, and peanut oil. Experts believe that some monounsaturated fats may help the body stay healthy by actually reducing cholesterol levels in the blood.

Polyunsaturated fats do not contribute to cholesterol problems. Safflower, corn, cottonseed, sunflower, sesame, and soybean oil all contain this type of fat. Polyunsaturated fats supply the body with a special type of fat called *linoleic acid.* About 3 grams (0.1 ounces) of linoleic acid a day are essential to a good, healthy body. The human body cannot produce linoleic acid. Humans must get this important acid by eating polyunsaturated fats that occur naturally in plants.

Saturated Fats	Unsaturated Fats
Butter	Canola oil
Cheese	Corn oil
Chocolate	Cottonseed oil
Cocoa butter	Fish
Coconut oil	Nuts
Cream	Olive oil
Eggs	Peanut oil
Hydrogenated shortening	Safflower oil
Ice cream	Soybean oil
Lard	Sunflower oil
Palm oil	
Red meat	
Whole milk	

FATTY FOODS

It's easy to tell that some foods have fats. Butter, oil, steak, and potato chips are all foods that you would expect to contain fat. But there are some foods with fats that might surprise you. Foods that contain hidden fats include peanut butter, doughnuts, nuts, cake, and milk.

Some foods have fats added to them to make them richer and more flavorful. Think of a baked potato without butter, a salad without dressing, or a ham sandwich without mayonnaise! Yet adding fats to our foods can have a high cost. Most of the fats the average American consumes each day are fats that have been added to foods.

Want to cut down on your fat intake? Try foods with little or no fat, such as fruits, vegetables, fish, poultry, and lean meats. Popcorn is another healthy snack, but hold the butter! You can also cut down on fat by choosing grilled, baked, or steamed foods instead of fried foods. Drinking low-fat milk can help, too.

QUESTIONS TO EXPLORE

- What are the six basic nutrients your body needs for growth and development?

- What are the important functions of fat in the body?

- What are some of the problems faced by people who have too much fat in their diets?

The Food Guide Pyramid

The Food Guide Pyramid teaches people which foods help them maintain a healthy, well balanced daily diet. The Food Guide Pyramid separates food into six basic groups. It is best to eat more foods from the base of the pyramid.

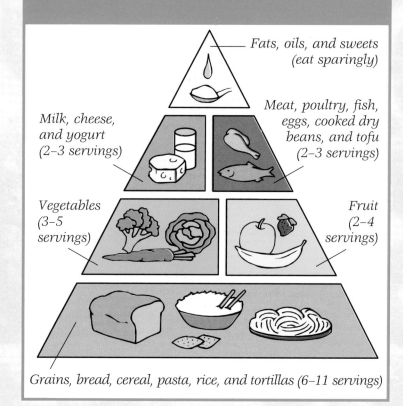

Fats, oils, and sweets (eat sparingly)

Meat, poultry, fish, eggs, cooked dry beans, and tofu (2–3 servings)

Milk, cheese, and yogurt (2–3 servings)

Vegetables (3–5 servings)

Fruit (2–4 servings)

Grains, bread, cereal, pasta, rice, and tortillas (6–11 servings)

A Healthy Career

Who decides exactly what a healthy, well balanced diet is? *Nutritionists* have that job. Nutritionists are people who study how food and diets affect the human body. They can help people who have special dietary needs. People who have diabetes, cancer, and heart disease can benefit from talking to a nutritionist. The nutritionist can assist them in planning diets that will help keep their bodies healthy.

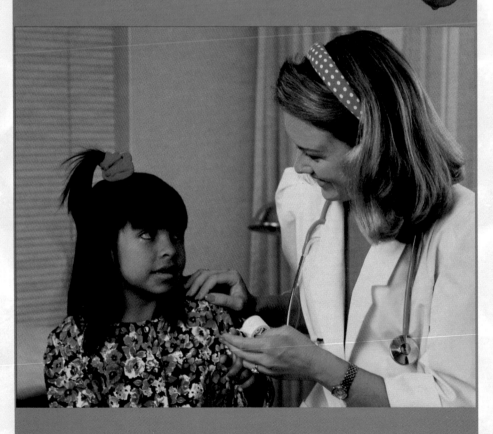

Your school probably has a nutritionist who makes sure school lunches are healthy *and* delicious. The nutritionist's job is to make sure you're getting meals that are well balanced, low in fat, and high in other nutrients. Your nutritionist knows that good eating habits start early!

THE DIGESTIVE SYSTEM

Different types of foods have the nutrients needed to make the body work. When first eaten, however, most foods are not in a form our bodies can use. It is the function of the *digestive system* to break down food, turning it into the materials the body must have to survive. The digestive system is a tube 9 meters (30 feet) long. It runs from the mouth to the rectum. There are several different sections of the digestive system.

Your digestive system is like an efficient food-processing factory. The digestive process begins the moment you put food into your mouth. It continues down the *esophagus,* into the *stomach,* then through the *intestines.* The process is finally finished when everything that cannot be used is passed from your body as *waste.*

What happens when you take a big bite of pepperoni pizza?

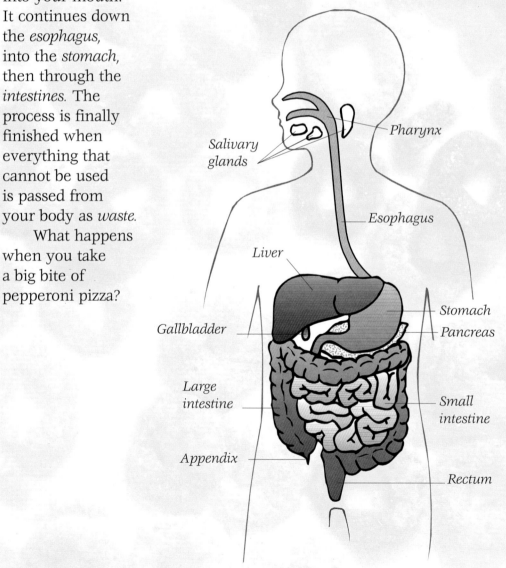

Pharynx

Salivary glands

Esophagus

Liver

Stomach

Pancreas

Gallbladder

Large intestine

Small intestine

Appendix

Rectum

THE MOUTH

The digestive process begins in the mouth when you take your first bite of pizza. Your teeth grind your food into small, easy-to-swallow pieces. *Saliva* inside your mouth softens and moistens the pizza pieces, making them even easier to swallow. Saliva contains a chemical known as an *enzyme.* The enzyme works to break down the starches in the pizza crust.

The only parts of the digestive process that you have control over are chewing and swallowing your food. After that, the entire digestive process takes place automatically.

THE ESOPHAGUS

After you swallow the chewed pizza, it enters the esophagus. The esophagus is a tube about 25 centimeters (10 inches) long. It runs through your chest, connecting the throat to the stomach. Muscles in the esophagus push the food down toward the stomach. This pushing, pumping movement is called *peristalsis.*

It takes just seconds for the food to travel down the esophagus. At the bottom of the esophagus, a valve made of muscle awaits. The valve is called a *sphincter.* The sphincter relaxes to allow food into the stomach. Then it tightens again to ensure that foods and acids do not escape from the stomach back into the esophagus.

THE STOMACH

The stomach is a pouchlike organ. Inside the stomach, the work of digesting food really gets going. Stomach muscles contract about every 20 seconds, squeezing and mashing everything inside. Bites of pizza are mixed together with liquids and digestive juices. The digestive juices contain stomach acid and another kind of enzyme. The acid breaks down and liquefies the food, while the enzyme breaks down proteins. By the time your stomach is through, the bite of pizza is virtually unrecognizable.

Once the pizza has been broken down and liquefied, it is pushed into the small intestine. There is another sphincter muscle located at the bottom of the stomach. It allows small amounts of food into the small intestine. Some nutrients move more slowly through the stomach than others. Fatty foods, for example, remain in the stomach much longer than other types of foods. Foods can remain in the stomach from 5 minutes to several hours.

7

THE SMALL INTESTINE

The small intestine is a twisting, turning tube 5 to 6 meters (16 to 20 feet) long. The tube is only 4 centimeters (1.6 inches) in diameter. Inside the small intestine, food is broken down into tiny molecules. Your body will eventually use the molecules for the energy it needs. In the small intestine, new digestive juices containing many different enzymes are added to the food. These juices break down carbohydrates, fats, and proteins in the cheese and other parts of the pizza.

Every square centimeter of the small intestine is lined with billions of tiny, fingerlike organs. These are called *villi*. After the food has been broken down, the villi absorb the nutrients and pass them into the bloodstream. They travel to organs and cells that need them all around the body.

It takes about 5 hours for the small intestine to perform its function. When it's done, all that is left of the pizza are materials that cannot be broken down and digested. The leftover, unusable substance is waste. Waste includes fiber, which cannot be digested by the body. After the small intestine has removed all the usable materials, the watery waste substance is sent into the large intestine.

THE LARGE INTESTINE

The large intestine is wider than the small intestine. At 1.5 meters (5 feet) in length, however, it is much shorter. In the large intestine, excess water and leftover minerals are removed from the waste. As the waste moves through the large intestine, it gradually becomes more solid. The digestive process ends when the solid waste is expelled from the body through the rectum. The whole digestive process can take from 12 hours to 2 days.

QUESTIONS TO EXPLORE

■ What organs make up your digestive system?

■ What function does each organ perform in the system?

■ How is the function of the small intestine different from the function of the large intestine?

Fascinating Facts about the Digestive System

■ What would happen if you stood on your head while you ate? The digestive process would still work. The muscles in your esophagus, stomach, and intestines keep the food moving in the direction it should go. Even in zero-gravity, astronauts have no problems digesting their food!

■ In a healthy adult, the small intestine absorbs 3.8 liters (1 gallon) of water every 24 hours. The 3.8 liters contain about 28 grams (1 ounce) of salt.

■ There are other organs that aid in the digestive process. These include the *liver*, the *gallbladder*, and the *pancreas*. The liver produces *bile* to break down fats and remove toxins from digested foods in the small intestine. The gallbladder stores bile from the liver so it can be released into the small intestine. The pancreas produces a number of enzymes that aid in the digestive process.

■ An adult stomach can hold about 1.9 liters (2 quarts).

■ Stomachaches may occur when the natural acids found in some foods combine with stomach acids. Too much acid irritates the stomach lining.

■ Adults produce about 1.7 liters (1.8 quarts) of saliva each day.

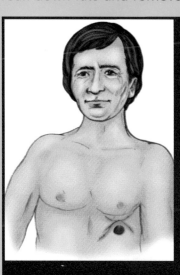

The Man with a Hole in His Stomach

In 1822, a young man living in Michigan suffered a terrible accident. Alexis St. Martin was cleaning his shotgun when the weapon went off. St. Martin was left with a gaping wound in his abdomen. Dr. William Beaumont was called in to treat the patient. He believed the man would be dead within hours.

St. Martin survived with a small hole 2 centimeters (0.8 inches) wide in his stomach. The hole never healed over. Over the next 10 years, Beaumont conducted many experiments on St. Martin. The experiments gave Beaumont and other doctors of the time important information about the digestive process.

Beaumont tied pieces of pork, beef, and other foods on strings. Then he lowered the foods directly into St. Martin's stomach. After varying amounts of time, the doctor would remove the foods from the stomach and examine the results. Beaumont also removed and studied stomach juices from St. Martin's stomach. In 1833, Beaumont published a book detailing his experiments. He became famous for his work.

As for Alexis St. Martin, he married, had several children, and lived to be 76 years old.

A SWEET STORY

Hey, you with the sweet tooth! Do you really scream for ice cream? Do you count the days until Halloween? Do your friends hide the chocolate when you come to visit? Then you're like millions of people through the centuries who have loved sugar.

Sugar is the sweet substance that is found naturally in many forms, in many foods. You probably don't think about it, but if you're eating something sweet, chances are that it has some type of sugar in it. The sugar we add to cereal or lemonade is a type of sugar called *sucrose*. Sucrose is also known as *refined sugar*.

Today refined sugar is plentiful. More than 100 million tons of refined sugar are produced every year. But sugar wasn't always so readily available. Hundreds of years ago, sugar was considered a valuable commodity, available only to royalty or the very wealthy.

SUGAR CANE: SUPER SWEET STORER

Although sucrose is produced by all green plants, refined sugar comes from just two sources: sugar cane and sugar beets. Most green plants convert sucrose into starch before storing it for energy. Sugar cane and sugar beets, however, do not change sucrose to starch. These two plants are the only ones that store large amounts of sucrose unchanged.

Sugar cane is a type of tropical plant that stores sugar in its stalk. Some historians believe that the first people to grow sugar cane for sucrose lived in the Polynesian Islands. Eventually people in India, China, and Arabia began growing sugar cane.

Sugar Time Line

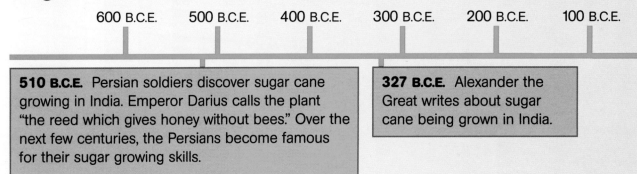

600 B.C.E.   500 B.C.E.   400 B.C.E.   300 B.C.E.   200 B.C.E.   100 B.C.E.

510 B.C.E. Persian soldiers discover sugar cane growing in India. Emperor Darius calls the plant "the reed which gives honey without bees." Over the next few centuries, the Persians become famous for their sugar growing skills.

327 B.C.E. Alexander the Great writes about sugar cane being grown in India.

When Europeans started colonizing the New World, they brought sugar cane cuttings with them. By the 1600s, sugar making was a profitable business in South and Central America.

Sugar cane was first planted in the United States in New Orleans, Louisiana, in the 1600s. By the 1830s, sugar making was a major industry in America. Today thriving cane sugar industries exist in Hawaii, Florida, Louisiana, Texas, and Puerto Rico.

REFINING SUGAR CANE

Turning sugar cane stalks into sugar is a process with many steps. Before the stalks can be harvested, they must be between 3 and 4 meters (10 and 13 feet) tall. The taller the sugar cane, the more sugar the plant will have inside. Once the sugar cane is ready, the stalk is cut close to the ground. In some places, workers cut the stalks with *machetes,* knives with big, broad blades. In other places, the sugar cane is harvested with machines. The roots are left in the ground to grow again the next year.

After cutting, the sugar cane stalks are taken to a sugar mill, where they are chopped and shredded. Next the cane is run through heavy rollers so that all the juice is squeezed out. This sugary juice is then purified through boiling. A thick syrup is left after

Harvesting mature sugar cane stalks in Barbados

the boiling. The syrup is placed into a special machine that spins rapidly, separating sugar crystals from a thick black syrup that

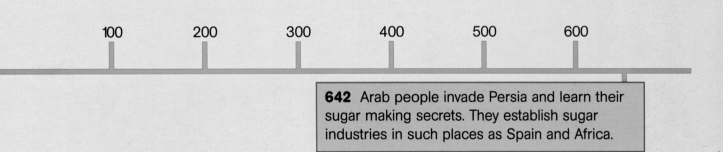

| 100 | 200 | 300 | 400 | 500 | 600 |

642 Arab people invade Persia and learn their sugar making secrets. They establish sugar industries in such places as Spain and Africa.

we know as *molasses*. The sugar crystals, coated with a thin layer of molasses, are light brown. This is *raw sugar*.

At this point, the raw sugar is shipped from the sugar mill to a factory called a *refinery*. At the refinery, the process of making sugar is completed. Here the raw sugar is washed, then soaked in a saturated sugar-water solution. The resulting syrup once again is placed in a machine that spins it rapidly. This time, the crystals are smaller and whiter. The more times the process is repeated, the smaller and finer the crystals are. Finally the substance once known as "white gold" is dried, packaged, and shipped away for sale. Refineries can process thousands of tons of sugar each day.

SUGAR BEETS

For many centuries, sugar cane was thought to be the only major source of sucrose. In the mid-1700s, however, German scientists discovered that sugar beets were also a good source for the sweet treat. Sugar beets are root vegetables, like carrots and radishes, that grow underground. They can store a lot of sucrose in their roots. Unlike sugar cane, which can only be grown in warm climates, sugar beets can be grown in colder areas. After a method of removing the sugar from sugar beets was invented in 1787, such countries as France, Austria-Hungary, and Russia began growing sugar beets for sucrose.

Using sugar beets, the first part of the sugar making process is different from that using sugar cane. First the beets must be dug out of the ground. Their roots are removed, washed, and sliced into thin strips. The roots are then boiled in water to

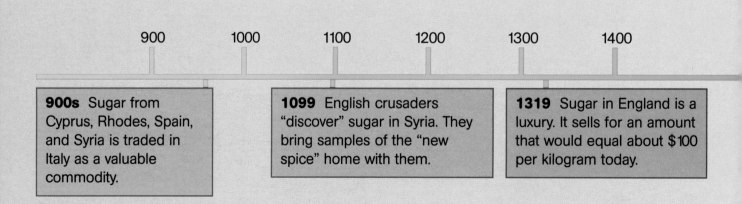

900   1000   1100   1200   1300   1400

900s Sugar from Cyprus, Rhodes, Spain, and Syria is traded in Italy as a valuable commodity.

1099 English crusaders "discover" sugar in Syria. They bring samples of the "new spice" home with them.

1319 Sugar in England is a luxury. It sells for an amount that would equal about $100 per kilogram today.

remove the sugar. After this, the process becomes very similar to sugar cane processing. The beet sugar juice is boiled, washed, and spun. The resulting beet sugar is identical to cane sugar.

In the United States, large crops of sugar beets are grown in California, Colorado, Idaho, Montana, and Nebraska. Today about one-third of all refined sugar in the U.S. comes from sugar beets.

ARTIFICIAL SWEETENERS

Ever wonder how some "diet" foods can taste so sweet? Many diet foods contain chemicals called *artificial sweeteners*. Some people with medical problems cannot have sugar in their diets. Others just want to cut down on how much sugar they eat each day. More than 100 years ago, scientists began looking for ways to sweeten foods without sugar.

The first artificial sweetener ever developed was *saccharine*. Saccharine, invented in 1879, became available to *diabetics* in 1900. Diabetics are people who cannot have sugar in their diets. Saccharine is more than 500 times sweeter than refined sugar. Food companies use saccharine in some sodas and other foods. In recent years, however, the Food and Drug Administration (FDA) has warned that saccharine can cause cancer in some animals.

One of the most recent artificial sweeteners to come into use is *aspartame*. Aspartame is a sugar substitute that was approved for use in 1981. Many people prefer aspartame to saccharine because it doesn't have the bitter aftertaste. Scientists are not yet sure whether aspartame is safe to consume in large quantities. Check the label on a package of artificial sweetener to see what it contains.

1500	1600	1700	1800	1900	2000

1493 Christopher Columbus brings sugar cane cuttings to the West Indies. The plants grow rapidly in the warm, tropical climate.

1747 The sugar beet is discovered to be a good source of sugar.

1802 The first sugar beet factory is founded in Kunern, Germany.

1879 Saccharine, an artificial sweetener, is developed.

1981 Aspartame, another artificial sweetener, is approved in the United States for use in foods.

SUGAR SMARTS

Like fats, sugars get a bad rap from health-conscious people. Sugars have been blamed for causing obesity, tooth decay, hyperactivity, depression, and diabetes. Some of these charges against sugar are true. Others are not. While an excess amount of sugar in your diet can be a bad thing, your body needs sugar. In fact, a well balanced diet includes some sugars.

Why are sugars important? They are your body's source for quick energy. Many foods naturally contain sugars. Others have sugars added to them to improve their taste or to act as preservatives. Whatever form they're in, sugars give your cells, muscles, and organs the power they need to work, play, and grow.

TYPES OF SUGAR

There are more than 100 different types of sugar. They are found in many different types of food. The names of most sugars end with the suffix -ose. When you see a food ingredient that ends with those letters, you'll know that the food has a form of sugar in it.

Sucrose is a sugar that is found in sugar cane and sugar beets. Sucrose is actually a complex sugar composed of two simple sugars, fructose and glucose.

Fructose is a sugar that is found naturally in fruits, vegetables, and honey. Fructose is the sweetest type of sugar.

Glucose is found in fruits and vegetables. It is also found in human blood. Glucose is less sweet than sucrose.

Pineapples contain fructose.

Maltose is a kind of sugar that is found in grains and other starches. Maltose can also be found in *corn syrup,* a substance used as a sweetener in many foods.

Lactose is a sugar that is found in milk.

14

YOUR BODY AND SUGAR

Starches can be found in pasta.

Sugars are simple carbohydrates. Carbohydrates are one of the six types of nutrients that your body must have. Starches are complex carbohydrates. They are found in foods such as bread, cereal, rice, and pasta.

Of all the types of sugar you might eat in a day, glucose is the only one that your cells can convert into energy. All other types of sugar must be broken down into glucose by the body before they can be used. Sugars and complex carbohydrates are broken down into glucose during the digestive process. Glucose then travels through the bloodstream to all of the body's cells.

In the cells, glucose is further broken down and converted into energy. This process is called *metabolism*. Energy from metabolism is used for every bodily function.

THE RIGHT AMOUNT OF SUGAR

There is no right or wrong amount of sugar in a daily diet. Most nutritionists recommend that people not eat too much sugar. Every gram of sugar you eat contains about 4 calories. Those calories are often called "empty calories." That means they lack other important nutrients that your body needs, such as vitamins and minerals. Eating a healthy, well balanced diet will give you all the sugars you need. Fruits, vegetables, cereals, and low-fat milk are all good sources of natural sugars.

When a person eats a diet that is high in sugar, health problems can result. Extra, unneeded sugar is stored in the body as fat. As a result, excess sugar intake can contribute to obesity. Sugar is also food for *plaque*, bacteria that live in your mouth. People who eat a lot of sugar and do not care for their teeth properly risk tooth decay and gum disease.

Although sugar has been blamed for causing hyperactivity and depression, research has not established any such connections. For many years, it was also thought that sugar caused diabetes. Although people with diabetes need to avoid sugars, doctors now know that sugars do not cause this condition.

LIVING WITH DIABETES

Diabetes is a disease that affects the body's ability to use glucose correctly. The *pancreas,* a large gland near the junction of the stomach and the small intestine, stops producing *insulin.* Insulin is one of the most important chemicals in our bodies. It acts in the liver and other parts of the body to control the amount of glucose in the blood. Without insulin, too much glucose builds up in the bloodstream. If not treated, diabetes can cause blindness, kidney disease, heart disease, coma, and even death.

Doctors aren't exactly sure what causes diabetes. Many believe that some people are more likely to get the disease because it runs in their families. Environmental "triggers" such as viruses may cause the onset of diabetes.

Diabetes affects people of all ages, including children. Most children with this disease have *Type I diabetes.* Type I diabetes is also known as *insulin-dependent diabetes.* Children with Type I diabetes must take insulin to survive. They must also carefully monitor the foods they eat in order to make sure that they don't have too much sugar in their blood.

Although their lives change, children who have diabetes can live happy, healthy lives. Robin and Jon Reitzes are a brother and sister who have been living with Type I diabetes since they were very young. Robin, 24, is a graduate student in New York. Jon, 20, is a college student in St. Louis, Missouri.

Robin Reitzes

Jon Reitzes

Q: *How old were you when you were diagnosed?*

RR: I was 13 months old when I was first diagnosed. At the time, I became very ill. I was vomiting, lethargic, and losing weight. I was put in the hospital and was very close to dying. Finally the diabetes was diagnosed.

JR: I was 8 months old when I was diagnosed. My mother recognized the symptoms and took me to the hospital.

Q: *How was your life different from other boys and girls?*

RR: I never felt any different from any of the other kids in school. I don't remember having a low blood sugar reaction in elementary school. As a child, I always knew when my blood sugar was going low. I had to have snack time, but so did the other kids. The only difference was not being able to eat cupcakes. Instead I would go to school with an apple.

JR: When I was very little, I never even thought about having diabetes. I think I started really thinking about it when I was in the second or third grade. I remember very clearly sitting on the counter and crying about it. But that was probably a result of my blood sugar being low.

Q: *When did you start giving yourself insulin shots?*

RR: Mom gave me my shots until I was 9 or 10. After that, I was glad to be able to take care of myself and be independent. Today I take about three or four shots a day.

JR: I was on my own with the insulin by the age of 8 or 9. Of course, my mom always checked to make sure everything was okay. We kept log books.

Q: *Is it difficult to give yourself insulin shots?*

JR: People always ask, "How can you do this? Doesn't it hurt?" You do it because you have to. It's going to save your life. People get up and brush their teeth, I just have another step.

Q: *Does exercise help you control your diabetes?*

RR: Exercise is the best thing that ever happened. It helps keep my blood sugar down, helps the insulin work more efficiently, and helps me [maintain a healthy] weight. I try to exercise 4 to 5 days a week.

JR: I was very active in high school. Wrestling, cross country, lacrosse. I never had high blood sugar when I was wrestling. Now that I'm in college, I have a high work load. But I still try to exercise whenever I can. I rollerblade or walk a couple of miles to class whenever possible. Everything works better, your mind and body, when you exercise.

Q: *What is your diet like? Do you have a nutrition plan?*

RR: I can eat all foods in moderation. For example, I'm having a little ice cream tonight because I exercised for 2 hours today. In my mind, I keep track of what I eat. The important thing is to keep my blood sugar at a normal, healthy level. The better I do this, the healthier I am.

JR: I pretty much eat what I like. But when food can make you sick, when eating ice cream can make you physically ill, sometimes you do it, a lot of times you don't. You look at food in a completely different way. Moderation is the key. You have to understand that there are immediate consequences to eating. I can live the life I want as long as I balance insulin, diet, and exercise.

Q: *What is the worst thing about having diabetes?*

RR: Where do I start? I think the worst thing is that I can't be spontaneous. I must know when to eat and when to exercise. I'm always on a schedule. I like to travel, but I worry about losing my insulin. I'm always double- and triple-checking my bag. In my pocketbook, I always have to carry my blood sugar monitor, insulin, syringes, and other stuff.

Q: *What would you like to tell kids who have diabetes?*

RR: Take good care of yourself. The more you neglect it, the worse you feel. A lot of kids in our town had it. You'd see kids not taking care of themselves, not doing their shots. That's when you see the worst cases. You can manage your diabetes and live a normal, healthy life.

JR: There are two ways to look at diabetes. You can view it as a challenge, with your goal being to become a healthy person. Or you can give up. You have to become master of yourself very early on. Don't waste time waiting for something to happen. Don't wait for a cure or hope for this or that. Take responsibility for yourself. Diabetes is a part of you, but it doesn't need to consume you.

Q: *How can kids without diabetes support those who do have this condition?*

RR: They should treat kids with diabetes normally. It's hard enough to be a kid with all the teasing that goes on. Diabetes is treatable, and it's not contagious.

JR: If your friend has diabetes, be sensitive to his needs if he's going to hang out with you. Nothing means more than a friend who is concerned, who takes a second out of his day to make sure everything is okay.

Breakthroughs in Medicine

Type I diabetes is a serious disease that can be controlled but not cured. An estimated 500,000 to 1 million people in America have Type I diabetes. Since 1921, when insulin was first isolated, medical breakthroughs have helped people with diabetes control this life-changing disease. Today medical advances continue to improve the lives of diabetics everywhere. Each year, more effective medicines and treatments help. Medical research sheds light on the causes and possible prevention of the disease. And scientists continue to work toward a cure for diabetes.

Take a Deep Breath One of the worst parts for children with diabetes is giving themselves shots of insulin several times a day. Now a new method of getting insulin has been developed. Diabetics can inhale a dry powder by mouth. The inhaled insulin goes directly into the lungs, then into the bloodstream.

Laser Beam People with diabetes have to use sharp instruments called *lancets* to prick their fingers for blood sugar tests. This sometimes painful procedure must be done from four to seven times a day. A recent innovation could make this a thing of the past. A new glucose monitor called the "Lasette" uses a laser beam to painlessly create a tiny hole in a person's finger.

Watch Your Blood Sugar Another innovation that is currently being tested is the "GlucoWatch." The GlucoWatch is a small, watch-sized device that is worn on the wrist. The patch on the back of the device automatically extracts and measures glucose up to three times an hour.

Moving Toward a Cure One cure for people who suffer from Type I diabetes is a pancreas transplant. Yet these transplants can be risky. Sometimes the body rejects the new gland. Today scientists are developing more effective and less harmful drugs to help the body accept a transplanted pancreas.

YOUR TERRIFIC TONGUE

The tongue is one of the most amazing muscles in your body. It helps you talk, chew, and swallow. Without the tongue, you wouldn't be able to taste a thing! *Taste buds*, thousands of tiny nerve endings located all over the tongue, do the trick. The taste buds can sense four different tastes. These are *sweet, sour, salty,* and *bitter.*

The taste buds that sense sweet foods are located on the tip of your tongue. Foods with sugars in them, such as ice cream, fruits, and cookies, taste sweet.

Salty foods are sensed by taste buds that are found on the sides of the tongue, toward the front. Salts make foods such as potato chips, hot dogs, and fried chicken taste salty.

Taste buds that sense sour foods can be found on the sides of the tongue, toward the back. Acids in lemons, vinegar, and pickles trigger your sour taste buds.

The taste buds that sense bitter foods are located at the back of the tongue. Bitter tastes include un-sweetened chocolate, coffee, and aspirin. People are most sensitive to bitter foods.

Some foods have combinations of different tastes. When you eat sweet-and-sour shrimp, your taste buds are getting a workout. They sense the sugar, as well as the vinegar, in the sauce. If you put soy sauce on your rice, then the taste buds that sense salt will also get some use.

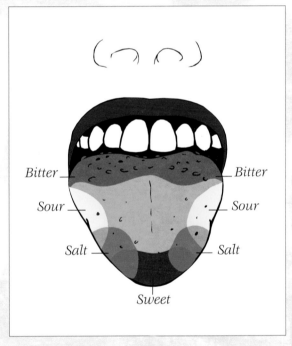

The tongue isn't the only part of the body involved in tasting, however. Nerve cells connected to the taste buds send messages to the brain, where taste is interpreted. Saliva produced by the glands carries the flavor over the taste buds. And even the nose plays a part in sensing taste. A food's smell helps your brain recognize what it is you're eating!

VITAMINS

A D-lightful Vitamin!

Vitamin D is a very important nutrient! Too little of it, and a body can develop *rickets*, a disease that causes bowed legs and other bone problems. Too much vitamin D can cause sickness and calcium buildup in the heart, lungs, and kidneys.

Vitamin D helps the body absorb calcium and phosphorous, two minerals that all people need for strong bones, teeth, and nails. Only a few foods contain vitamin D. These foods include butter, eggs, fish liver oils, margarine, fortified milk, and oily fishes such as tuna, herring, and salmon.

Food is not the only way we get vitamin D. Sometimes vitamin D is referred to as the "sunshine vitamin." That's because it is the only vitamin produced by skin cells in response to sunlight. Vitamin D is produced when cholesterol in skin cells reacts to the Sun's ultraviolet rays.

It takes very little exposure to sunlight for our skin cells to make all the vitamin D we need for one day. However, we can never get too much vitamin D from the Sun. The body regulates vitamin D production in the skin cells to make sure this doesn't happen. Older people who are less active outdoors in the sunlight need to be sure they get enough vitamin D in their diets.

DISCOVERING VITAMIN D

The first evidence of a nutrient that contributed to healthy bones was announced in 1919 by British scientist Sir Edward Mellanby. That year, Mellanby began experimenting with dogs. He kept the dogs indoors and fed them a diet of oatmeal. The dogs soon developed rickets.

Mellanby found that by adding cod liver oil to the oatmeal, he could cure the dogs. This was the first time anyone had suggested that rickets might be caused by not getting enough of a nutrient. Parents everywhere began feeding their children capsules and spoonfuls of cod liver oil.

Dr. E.V. McCollum took Mellanby's research one step further. McCollum had already isolated vitamin A from cod liver oil. In 1922, he discovered a new nutrient in cod liver oil that he called vitamin D. With the discovery of vitamin D, nutritionists around the world gained an important weapon in the fight against rickets. The vitamin was soon being added to such foods as milk and margarine. When you look on a milk label and see the words "Vitamin D fortified," you'll now know how important that is!

Vitamins

Vitamins are natural substances that help the body work properly and stay healthy. Vitamins are essential nutrients. They aid in growth and promote healthy skin, hair, eyes, and other parts of the body. Humans must have small amounts of vitamins in their daily diets in order to stay healthy.

There are 13 different types of vitamins. The body cannot make most of its own vitamins. Therefore, people must get vitamins from the foods they eat. As long as people enjoy healthy, well balanced diets, they will get plenty of vitamins from the foods they eat. However, if people don't get enough vitamins in their diets, health problems can result. Vitamin deficiencies can cause serious diseases that sometimes even lead to death.

In recent years, many people have begun taking vitamin supplements. Some groups of people such as pregnant women, infants, children, and people who are ill may need supplements. But for most people, nutritionists believe that vitamin supplements are unnecessary. We get the small amounts of vitamins we need from the foods we eat. In addition, taking excess amounts of vitamins may lead to health problems. An excess of vitamin A, for example, can stunt growth and cause nausea, hair loss, skin rashes, and enlargement of the liver. An excess of vitamin D can cause headaches, diarrhea, and nausea, as well as increased levels of calcium in the blood and urine, or even kidney damage.

Vitamins are divided into two groups. These are *fat-soluble* and *water-soluble.* Fat-soluble vitamins only dissolve in fats and oils. Water-soluble vitamins only dissolve in water.

Vitamin supplements

Fat-Soluble Vitamins

Vitamin A	Promotes healthy skin, hair, and eyes. It is found in broccoli, carrots, spinach, eggs, dairy products, and liver.
Vitamin D	Helps the body use calcium for stronger bones and teeth. It is found in milk, eggs, and fish liver oils. Vitamin D is also produced by skin cells when they are exposed to sunlight.
Vitamin E	Helps make muscle tissue and protects cells from damage. It is found in most foods.
Vitamin K	Helps blood clot and keeps bones healthy. It is found in vegetables, egg yolks, liver, and fish oils. It is also produced by intestinal bacteria.

Water-Soluble Vitamins

*There are eight B complex vitamins.

Vitamin B1* *(Thiamin)*	Helps the body get energy from carbohydrates. It can be found in dairy foods, whole grains, eggs, and beans.
Vitamin B2* *(Riboflavin)*	Helps cells use oxygen and keeps skin healthy. It is found in cheese, eggs, milk, leafy vegetables, liver, fish, and meat.
Vitamin B3* *(Niacin)*	Helps cells work properly and keeps skin healthy. It is found in grains, fish, meat, peanuts, and leafy vegetables.
Vitamin B5* *(Pantothenic acid)*	Helps the body turn food into energy. It is found in nearly all foods. It is also produced by intestinal bacteria.
Vitamin B6* *(Pyridoxine)*	Helps the body convert proteins and fats into energy. It is found in eggs, grains, nuts, fish, liver, and poultry.
Vitamin B12*	Necessary for red blood cell production and a healthy nervous system. It is found in eggs, dairy products, fish, poultry, and meat.
Folic acid*	Promotes the production of red blood cells. It is found in fruits, beans, and vegetables.
Biotin*	Helps the body get energy from carbohydrates and helps form fatty acids. It is found in eggs, liver, and nuts.
Vitamin C *(Ascorbic acid)*	Promotes healthy skin, bones, muscles, and teeth. Also helps wounds heal more quickly. It is found in citrus fruits, tomatoes, potatoes, and strawberries.

THE SCOURGE OF SEAFARERS

Hundreds of years ago, *scurvy* was a deadly disease feared by seamen around the world. Scurvy made even the hardiest of sailors weak and unable to work. Sailors watched helplessly as sores erupted on their skin. Further, their teeth began to loosen because of gum disease. On long voyages, two out of every three sailors might die from scurvy.

Scurvy was a problem for people as long ago as 1500 B.C.E. The ancient Greeks and Romans wrote about the disease. During Ferdinand Magellan's round-the-world journey from 1519 to 1522, many of his crew members died of scurvy. In 1600, a British report stated that in the past 20 years, about 10,000 seamen had died because of the disease.

Centuries ago, no one knew what caused this mysterious illness. It was known that scurvy was connected to the sailors' diets. There were no problems while eating fresh foods on shore. But no one knew what exactly was missing from the diets at sea to cause the problems. And on long ocean voyages, keeping fresh food on board was impossible.

Today doctors know that scurvy is caused by a lack of *ascorbic acid*, also known as vitamin C. How did they find out?

FIRST STEPS TOWARD A CURE

The first step in treating and preventing scurvy came in 1747. James Lind (1716–1794) was a naval surgeon aboard a British ship sailing from England to Massachusetts. When 12 sailors came down with scurvy, Lind decided to try an experiment. He separated the sailors into six groups of two. All of the sailors ate the same foods for breakfast, lunch, and dinner. But each group received a different supplement.

James Lind

- Group 1 received a quart of apple cider each day.
- Group 2 received 25 drops of an elixir made with sulfuric acid and spices.
- Group 3 received two spoonfuls of vinegar three times a day.

- Group 4 received a mixture made up of different herbs and spices.
- Group 5 received a half-pint of sea water daily.
- Group 6 received two oranges and a lemon each day.

The sailors who received the citrus fruits got better right away. Lind believed that something in the fruits was making the men better. He was not sure exactly what it was. He gave the others oranges and lemons, and they began to recover also. After Lind's discovery, the British began to stock fresh fruit, as well as lemon juice and lime juice, on all sea voyages. Soon British sailors became known as "limeys."

It wasn't until 1932 that a Hungarian scientist discovered vitamin C. Then people knew what it was about limes and other citrus fruits that cured scurvy.

VITAMIN C

Vitamin C is an important part of a healthy diet. It helps heal cuts, bruises, and other wounds. Vitamin C also helps your body build healthy teeth, gums, and bones. When you are sick, your body uses vitamin C to fight infections. Vitamin C also helps your body more effectively absorb iron.

Citrus fruits

Humans, apes, and guinea pigs are the only mammals that cannot make vitamin C in the body. We must get vitamin C from the foods we eat. Foods that are high in vitamin C include such citrus fruits as oranges, lemons, and limes, as well as broccoli, tomatoes, potatoes, strawberries, and peppers. It is important to eat foods with vitamin C each day because the body cannot store it.

Although some people believe that taking large doses of vitamin C can prevent colds and more serious health problems, this has not been proven true. In fact, some researchers believe that taking large doses of vitamin C can be harmful to your health.

QUESTIONS TO EXPLORE

- What was the disease that plagued sailors at sea?
- What were the symptoms of the disease?
- How was a cure found for this disease?

LINUS PAULING

Linus Pauling was born in Oregon in 1901. He started his scientific career in the field of chemistry. He soon became a world-renowned expert on chemical bonds and the structures of molecules and crystals. Pauling also conducted important research on blood and proteins. In 1949, he showed that *sickle-cell anemia* is caused by abnormally shaped red blood cells. Sickle-cell anemia is a serious disease that often affects African Americans. Pauling was also interested in the effects of vitamin C on human health.

Linus Pauling, two-time Nobel prize-winner, holding an orange and a large model of a vitamin C molecule

After World War II (1939–1945), Pauling became concerned with the danger of nuclear arms testing. In 1958, Pauling presented the United Nations with a petition signed by 11,000 scientists warning of the dangers of nuclear testing. His anti-nuclear stand cost him his job. He lost many of his friends and supporters.

In 1973, Pauling founded the Linus Pauling Institute of Science and Medicine. Here Pauling conducted more important research. Much of it was on the benefits of vitamins. One of his favorite topics was the benefits of vitamin C. Pauling believed that large doses of the vitamin could help cure the common cold. He also believed that vitamin C might help fight cancer.

Pauling was a controversial figure. He was attacked by many who disagreed with his claims about vitamin C. Today medical research has not proven many of his claims about the vitamin. There is some evidence, however, that vitamin C may help fight cholesterol-related heart disease.

Linus Pauling and other recipients of the 1962 Nobel prize

Pauling was twice honored with a Nobel prize. He received his first Nobel prize for chemistry in 1954. This prize recognized his work with chemical bonding. In 1962, Pauling was awarded the Nobel Peace Prize. He died in 1994 at the age of 93.

FOOD LABELS

Ever wonder what the difference is between fruit juice and fruit drink? You can find out by reading food labels. Food labels can help you have a healthier diet. Although these labels might seem confusing, they're actually quite simple to read once you know what to look for.

What's on a food label? According to U.S. law, companies must include a food's ingredients, nutritional value, and number of calories per serving on all packaging. This allows consumers to know exactly what they're getting when they purchase their foods, and whether the foods fit into their diets.

UNDERSTANDING INGREDIENTS

For some people, reading a list of ingredients on a label can be a matter of life or death. Many people have food allergies. If they eat certain types of food, they may become sick or even die. For example, people who have diabetes need to know what's in their foods. They need to avoid foods that are high in sugars and other carbohydrates. Here's how ingredient lists can help *you* become food smart.

Check the main ingredients. Ingredients must be listed in order by mass, from largest quantity to smallest quantity. The first substance listed is the main ingredient.

Identify the sugars. Look for words that end in -ose. These are sugars.

Find the fats. Oil, butter, eggs, and lard are all fats.

Potato Chips

Nutrition Facts

Serving Size 50g (1.75 oz.)

Amount Per Serving

Calories	270
Calories from Fat	160

	% Daily Value*
Total Fat 17g	27%
Saturated Fat 5g	26%
Cholesterol 0mg	0%
Sodium 320mg	13%
Total Carbohydrate 26g	9%
Dietary Fiber 1g	4%
Sugars 0g	
Protein 3g	

Vitamin A	0%
Vitamin C	15%
Calcium	0%
Iron	2%

* Percent Daily Values are based on a 2,000 calorie diet. Your daily values may be higher or lower depending on your calorie needs.

		Calories	2,000	2,500
Total Fat	Less than		65g	80g
Sat Fat	Less than		20g	25g
Cholesterol	Less than		300g	300g
Sodium	Less than		2,400mg	2,400mg
Potassium			3,500mg	3,500mg
Total Carbohydrate			300g	375g
Dietary Fiber			25g	30g

Calories per gram:
Fat 9   *   Carbohydrate 4   *   Protein 4

Ingredients: Potatoes, vegetable oil (one or more of the following: corn, cottonseed, or sunflower), and salt. No preservatives.

Be aware of additives. Additives are any substances that are added to a food. Some additives are good for you, but others may not be so good for you. Some additives enhance flavor, while others act as preservatives. Vitamins and minerals are sometimes added to foods to make them healthier to eat.

IS IT GOOD FOR YOU?

Nutrition Information can be found on every food package. It includes information about what nutrients a food contains and how much. Nutrients listed are fat, cholesterol, sodium, carbohydrates, and protein. The label also includes the *Percent Daily Value.* That's the amount of each nutrient someone eating either a 2,000- or 2,500-calorie diet should have each day. Here are some tips to help you read the food label.

Check the serving size. All of the nutritional information is based on one serving of the food, not the entire package. The *serving size* is the amount of food customarily eaten at one sitting. For example, one serving of ice cream might be 106 grams (one-half cup). Serving size is listed in both metric and English measures.

Count the calories. The food label gives you two important

Frozen Pizza

Nutrition Facts

Serving Size 120g (4 oz.)

Amount Per Serving	
Calories	**320**
Calories from Fat	120

	% Daily Value*
Total Fat 14g	**22%**
Saturated Fat 6g	**30%**
Cholesterol 30mg	**10%**
Sodium 860mg	**36%**
Total Carbohydrate 33g	**11%**
Dietary Fiber 2g	**8%**
Sugars 7g	
Protein 16g	

Vitamin A	10%
Vitamin C	0%
Calcium	20%
Iron	6%

* Percent Daily Values are based on a 2,000 calorie diet. Your daily values may be higher or lower depending on your calorie needs.

	Calories	2,000	2,500
Total Fat	Less than	65g	80g
Sat Fat	Less than	20g	25g
Cholesterol	Less than	300g	300g
Sodium	Less than	2,400mg	2,400mg
Potassium		3,500mg	3,500mg
Total Carbohydrate		300g	375g
Dietary Fiber		25g	30g

Calories per gram:
Fat 9　＊　Carbohydrate 4　＊　Protein 4

Ingredients: **Crust:** Flour, water, sugar, cornmeal, vital wheat gluten, soybean or corn oil, yeast, salt, sodium bicarbonate, sodium aluminum phosphate, diacetyl tartaric acid, esters of mono- and diglycerides, sodium stearoyl, lactylate, and ascorbic acid.
Topping: Low-moisture, part-skim mozzarella cheese, pepperoni (pork, beef, salt, spices, lactic acid, sodium nitrite, BHA, BHT, citric acid, dextrose), tomato paste, water, parmesan, romano, and asiago cheeses, powdered cellulose (anti-caking agent), salt, soybean or corn oil, spices, and garlic.

calorie counts. These are *total calories* and *calories from fat*. A serving of potato chips, for example, may have 270 total calories and 160 calories from fat. More than 50 percent of the calories in this snack are from fat!

Figure out the fat content. What kind of fat are you eating? Saturated fats are the "bad" fats. Remember, unsaturated fats are better, but you should avoid eating foods high in either type of fat.

Watch for cholesterol and sodium. It's best to avoid foods that are high in either one of these substances.

Check the carbohydrates. It's important to be aware of the amount of carbohydrates you're getting in each serving.

Note the vitamins and minerals. If a food contains any vitamins and minerals, you'll find them listed here.

Mystery Food

Check out the ingredients of this food. Can you guess what it is? Check your answer on page 42.

Nutrition Facts

Serving Size 31g (~1 oz.)

Amount Per Serving

Calories	**190**
Calories from Fat	130

	% Daily Value*
Total Fat 16g	**25%**
Saturated Fat 3g	**16%**
Cholesterol 0mg	**0%**
Sodium 50mg	**2%**
Total Carbohydrate 6g	**2%**
Dietary Fiber 2g	**9%**
Sugars 2g	
Protein 8g	

Vitamin A	0%
Vitamin E	10%
Calcium	0%
Iron	4%
Riboflavin	2%
Niacin	20%

* Percent Daily Values are based on a 2,000 calorie diet. Your daily values may be higher or lower depending on your calorie needs.

	Calories	2,000	2,500
Total Fat	Less than	65g	80g
Sat Fat	Less than	20g	25g
Cholesterol	Less than	300g	300g
Sodium	Less than	2,400mg	2,400mg
Potassium		3,500mg	3,500mg
Total Carbohydrate		300g	375g
Dietary Fiber		25g	30g

Calories per gram:
Fat 9 * Carbohydrate 4 * Protein 4

Ingredients: Peanuts, partially hydrogenated vegetable oil (soybean), fully hydrogenated vegetable oils (rapeseed and soybean), mono- and diglycerides, molasses, sugar, and salt.

HEALTHY EATING, INTERNATIONAL STYLE

When you think of American food, what do you think of? Apple pie, french fries, and hamburgers are just a few foods that we consider "American." Now think about the foods you eat when you go to Italian, Chinese, or Mexican restaurants. Why doesn't everybody eat the same types of foods?

The kinds of foods eaten in different nations depend upon the geography and climate of an area. The geography and climate of Scotland, for example, are perfect for growing oats and barley. In Mexico, on the other hand, the climate is right for growing *maize*, or corn. If people live by the seaside, they are likely to have a diet high in fish. But those living in the mountains may not have access to fresh seafood.

Cultural beliefs and traditions also play important parts in dietary practices. In India, for example, some people do not eat beef. Others will not eat garlic and onions. In some cultures, it is against tradition to eat pork.

YOU EAT WHAT?

Some foods that we would find unappealing have important nutritional value in other cultures. Some native people of the far north, for example, eat raw whale and seal fat. In the cold winter months, fresh fruits and vegetables are not available. Without the vitamin C this fat provides, the people might develop scurvy. If they cook the fat, the vitamin C is lost.

Some cultures include insects in their diets. This may sound unappetizing to us. However, the insects are an important source of protein and vitamins in the diet. Additionally, insects are plentiful, easy to find, and cheaper to raise than cattle or other livestock. There are hundreds of kinds of edible bugs. These include mealworms, crickets, beetles, cicadas, and ants.

FOOD CULTURES AROUND THE WORLD

Some nutritionists believe that Americans could have much healthier diets if we patterned our meals after some other cultures. Mediterranean, Asian, and Latin American cultures, for example, have lower intakes of red meat and higher intakes of grains, fruits, and vegetables.

Mediterranean Region

The Mediterranean region includes such areas as Italy, Greece, Spain, and Portugal. Although different parts of the Mediterranean have their own distinct food styles, they all share some basic ingredients. Grains are an important part of Mediterranean diets. In Italy, for example, pasta is used in many recipes.

The Mediterranean diet has few animal fats. Instead olive oil is the main source of fat. Olive oil is mostly unsaturated fat, as opposed to animal fats, which are mostly saturated fats. Nutritionists say that mono-unsaturated fats are healthier for humans than saturated fats are.

Other important parts of Mediterranean diets include breads, such fresh vegetables as artichokes and eggplants, and fruit. Red meat is eaten only a few times a month, while chicken and fish are eaten a few times a week.

Latin America

Latin America includes Mexico and countries in Central and South America. Grains, fruits, and vegetables are all important parts of many Latin American diets. The chief grain is maize. Potatoes, peanuts, and dry beans are other important sources of protein.

Fast Food Chains

What do you do when you're on the run and need to eat a fast meal? Many of us stop into fast food restaurants. There are thousands of fast food restaurants in the United States. Fast food chains are quickly gaining in popularity around the world, too. In recent years, such countries as China and Russia have had chains spring up, especially in large towns and cities.

Fast food is not harmful to your health. However, you should be careful how much fast food you eat. Fast food meals are generally high in fat and sodium. They usually have few grains, fruits, or vegetables. Therefore, they are low in fiber, vitamins, and minerals. It does not hurt to have an occasional burger and fries. But it is more important to be more concerned with a healthy, well balanced diet overall.

Many fast food chains are aware that people today are more health-conscious than ever. Some offer more healthy choices for those who want to eat more nutritious meals. The next time you visit a fast food restaurant, think about trying a meal that is lower in fat and higher in other nutrients.

Much of the fat in many Latin American diets comes from such natural sources as fruits, nuts, and some high-fat vegetables like avocados. As with the Mediterranean diet, red meats are eaten only occasionally. Poultry and fish are eaten more regularly, perhaps a few times a week.

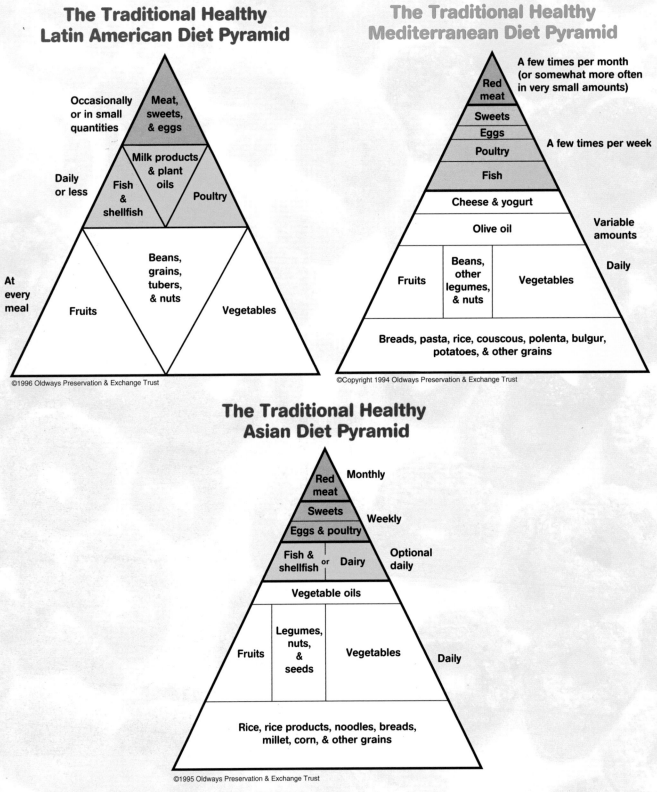

The Traditional Healthy Latin American Diet Pyramid

Occasionally or in small quantities — Meat, sweets, & eggs

Daily or less — Milk products & plant oils / Fish & shellfish / Poultry

At every meal — Fruits / Beans, grains, tubers, & nuts / Vegetables

©1996 Oldways Preservation & Exchange Trust

The Traditional Healthy Mediterranean Diet Pyramid

Red meat — A few times per month (or somewhat more often in very small amounts)

Sweets
Eggs
Poultry — A few times per week
Fish

Cheese & yogurt
Olive oil — Variable amounts

Fruits / Beans, other legumes, & nuts / Vegetables — Daily

Breads, pasta, rice, couscous, polenta, bulgur, potatoes, & other grains

©Copyright 1994 Oldways Preservation & Exchange Trust

The Traditional Healthy Asian Diet Pyramid

Red meat — Monthly
Sweets — Weekly
Eggs & poultry
Fish & shellfish **or** Dairy — Optional daily

Vegetable oils

Fruits / Legumes, nuts, & seeds / Vegetables — Daily

Rice, rice products, noodles, breads, millet, corn, & other grains

©1995 Oldways Preservation & Exchange Trust

Asia

Asia includes such countries as China, Thailand, Vietnam, Japan, and Korea. The Asian diet may be one of the healthiest. It is low in total fat and high in other nutrients. Rice is a feature in the Asian diet. This grain is a good source of carbohydrates, protein, fiber, minerals, and vitamins. People who live in Asia get from 25 percent to 80 percent of their total calories from rice each day. In China, the average person eats about 109 kilograms (243 pounds) of rice per year.

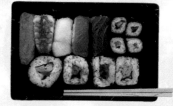

Other important ingredients in Asian diets include noodles and beans. They also include vegetables, nuts, and oils from these foods. Most Asian countries have no dairy products. There is also little red meat or pork eaten. People living near the sea have plenty of fresh fish in their diets.

America: Food from the Melting Pot

Before the arrival of colonists from Europe, the first Americans depended upon such staples as corn, beans, and squash. Native recipes often included these ingredients. Once the colonists did arrive, the Native Americans often taught them how to make use of these easy-to-grow ingredients. Such foods as cornbread, squash pie, and baked beans are examples of how settlers used these new foods.

Many of the foods that we have come to think of as important parts of an American diet today had their roots in countries far across the sea. That's because the United States is a nation of immigrants. The people who came from all over the world to make their homes here brought their food traditions and preferences with them. In many cases, such ethnic foods as lasagna, tacos, and egg rolls made their ways into the larger culture.

Breakfast around the World

What is your breakfast like? Compare a typical American breakfast to other breakfast meals around the world.

United States Orange juice, coffee, scrambled eggs, whole wheat toast with jam, bacon, home fries, slice of melon

China Rice, vegetables

Egypt Bean cakes with jam, eggs, pickles, cheese

France Coffee with milk, croissants with butter and jam

Greece Rolls, fresh fruit with yogurt, black coffee

Russia Tea, black bread, sausages, fried eggs, pickles

Turkey Soup, cheese pastry, wheat bread, black olives

FINDING A CAUSE FOR RICKETS

Scientists are curious about many things. They wonder about the world and how it works. To get answers to their questions, they make careful observations and look for patterns that might provide explanations. Sometimes they take measurements and look for patterns in the numbers. Sometimes they just count things and try to organize the counts in ways that might give answers to their questions. Scientists have many ways to learn about the world.

Once a scientist wondered about childhood illnesses. There are some illnesses that young children get that adults do not get very often. The scientist wondered why and wanted to find the causes of these illnesses.

He listed three of the most common illnesses in children. His list included *mumps, measles,* and *rickets.*

Mumps gives children painful swellings in their glands, usually the salivary glands that are to the sides of the jaw. When children get mumps, they have fevers, headaches, and problems swallowing.

Measles gives children a red rash that covers their whole bodies. These children get fevers, and they cough a lot.

Children with rickets have weak bones. Their bones swell in certain places, usually at the ribs or knees. The bones may bow or bend. They may become brittle and easily broken.

To the scientist, these childhood illnesses were very serious. Since no one knew much about them, he decided to first gather data about where the three illnesses occurred. His data came mainly from small villages in European countries.

After he got his information from doctors, the scientist sorted the data by geographic location. He considered countries such as Norway to be "high-latitude" countries. For his purposes, a high-latitude country was one that was near the North Pole. Countries such as Germany were considered "mid-latitude" countries. Countries near the equator were "low-latitude" countries. The scientist thought that children nearer the North Pole might get the illnesses more often than children near the equator. He thought his data would reflect this.

When he looked at this arrangement of his data, he could not find a pattern. Children at high, middle, and low latitudes seemed to get all three diseases at about the same rate.

The scientist thought about other factors that might be studied. He decided to see if there was any difference between children living in villages on high mountains, on the slopes of mountains, or in the deep valleys between mountains. He thought that the elevations where children lived might have something to do with the illnesses.

He rearranged his data to include the elevation factor. His charted data looked like this.

	Where children lived	Number of children with mumps	Number of children with rickets	Number of children with measles
HIGH ELEVATION	High mountains at low latitudes	46	14	38
	High mountains at middle latitudes	43	12	33
	High mountains at high latitudes	43	12	38
MEDIUM ELEVATION	Hillside slopes at low latitudes	41	12	34
	Hillside slopes at middle latitudes	44	15	36
	Hillside slopes at high latitudes	44	11	37
LOW ELEVATION	Deep mountain valleys at low latitudes	44	84	39
	Deep mountain valleys at middle latitudes	45	85	36
	Deep mountain valleys at high latitudes	45	89	34

The scientist was surprised at what he saw when he looked at the new data. See if you can recognize the pattern the scientist saw.

There was no pattern in the numbers for mumps or measles. But the scientist saw a pattern that told him something about rickets. Rickets showed up in high numbers when children lived in deep mountain valleys. It did not matter if the valleys were at low, middle, or high latitudes.

The discovery was an important one because it led other scientists toward studying the cause for this pattern. They found it was not the elevation that made the difference, but rather the lack of sunlight. High mountain villages (high elevations) receive a great deal of sunlight throughout the day. Hillside slopes (medium elevations) receive a fair amount of sunlight. But deep valleys between mountains (low elevations) are in the shadows of mountains for most of the day.

Today we know that sunlight causes our bodies to produce vitamin D naturally. Young children who get enough sunlight, eat foods containing vitamin D, or take vitamin D supplements do not get rickets. Doctors have found that the vitamin helps the body use calcium to build bones and keep them strong.

Since the time of this study, other scientists and doctors have found that mumps and measles are caused by viruses, and both are contagious. Today children can be vaccinated to prevent these two diseases.

Patterns in data can often lead to new discoveries or break-throughs. Perhaps some-day you will make an important discovery by looking for patterns in data.

This severely bowlegged child shows the symptoms of rickets.

HEALTHY KIDS

JUNE 2000   VOLUME 3, ISSUE 10

From the Editor:

Hello, everybody! It's time for another issue of Healthy Kids, *your favorite wellness newsletter. Here at Washington Middle School, we're committed to helping kids stay healthy. So in this issue, we'll check out a bunch of neat stories about kids' nutrition and health. We've also got the results of our poll from the last issue. So don't be afraid to take a big bite of this month's issue. It's low in fat, but high in other important nutrients!*

Poll Results

Last month, we asked the question that was on everybody's mind. "What's your favorite snack food?" Well, Washington Middle Schoolers, you might be surprised by the results. Here they are.

HERE'S NEXT MONTH'S POLL QUESTION:

How many hours a day do you usually spend watching TV?

Health Tip of the Month

If you're looking for a quick way to cut down on fats and sweets in your diet, try this. **Don't snack on cookies and potato chips. Instead choose plain popcorn, pretzels, low-fat yogurt, or a piece of fruit.**

HERE'S TO YOUR HEALTH!

Are you eating a healthy, well balanced diet? One way to find out is to keep your very own food diary. All you need is a notebook, or even a few pieces of paper stapled together. For 1 week, write down everything you eat. (Don't forget that candy bar you ate before dinner!)

Once you've recorded your meals and snacks, you can check to see how well you're doing. A healthy daily diet includes the following.

Bread, cereal, rice, or pasta

(6 to 11 servings)

Vegetables (3 to 5 servings)

Fruit (2 to 4 servings)

Milk, yogurt, or cheese (2 to 3 servings)

Meat, poultry, fish, dry beans, eggs, or nuts (2 to 3 servings)

Fats, oils, and sweets (eat sparingly)

Remember, eating a variety of different foods is important. Another way to keep your body at its best is to get plenty of exercise.

Ask Mrs. M

Dear Mrs. M,

What's the difference between drinks that are labeled "100 percent fruit juice" and those that are labeled "fruit drink"?

—Wondering at Washington Middle School

Dear Wondering,

That's a good question. Many people are fooled when they buy juices and juice drinks. They may not read the labels carefully, or they may not understand the differences between the products. Bottles of juice that are labeled "100 percent fruit juice" are just that. They are made completely of fruit juice. Bottles that do not say this contain other ingredients. These may be sweeteners, artificial and natural flavors, or artificial colors. The healthy, nutritious way to go is with 100 percent fruit juice. Now you know!

TV and Junk Food:
What's the Connection?

Did you know that the average kid spends 24 hours a week watching television? It's true! And that doesn't even count the hours spent surfing the 'Net or playing video games. The more time we spend in front of the TV, the less time we have for fun physical activities. In fact, by the time the average person turns 24, he or she has spent the equivalent of 3 years watching TV. That's equal to about 18,000 hours of being a couch potato.

Now think about this. When you're sitting in front of the TV, what do you like to do? Most kids (and some parents, too) like to munch on snacks. We all know a little snack food is okay. But some kids who snack in front of the TV end up eating way too much junk food. They eat potato chips, cookies, and other things. While watching TV, some kids don't pay attention to when they've had enough. They just keep snacking away! That's where problems can start.

Recent research has shown that there may be a link between kids who are overweight and the number of hours spent watching TV. In 1998, a study of more than 4,000 kids found that the more time spent in front of the TV, the more overweight kids were. Kids who are watching more TV are getting less exercise and snacking on junk foods. In addition, researchers noted that about 80 percent of advertisements during kids' shows are for food.

So before you sit down and space out, think twice. Instead why not walk the dog, do some sit-ups, or go for a bike ride? Your body will thank you later!

THINK ABOUT IT

What kinds of food ads do you think kids see while they're watching TV? Do you think the ads are for healthy foods?

·RECIPE OF THE MONTH·
HEALTHY TRAIL MIX

This easy snack was submitted by sixth grader Becca Joshua. It's a way-cool treat. You don't need to cook anything, and it tastes great.

Ingredients
Toasted oat cereal
Dried cranberries
Raisins
Walnuts
Banana chips
Carob chips

Directions
Put the ingredients in a plastic or brown paper bag. Shake them up until they are well mixed.

THE DANGERS OF DIETING

Most kids our age don't need diets. We actually need more nutrients than adults do. That's because we're still growing. Quick diets that are popular at the moment can be dangerous. You can lose muscle along with fat! People who use these "crash" diets usually end up gaining back all the weight they lost.

Some people who try to lose weight all the time develop eating disorders. People with eating disorders may starve themselves to death. They believe they look fat even when they aren't overweight.

If you are thinking about going on a diet, the best thing to do is talk to your doctor. If your doctor thinks you should lose some weight, he or she will help you. The doctor will tell you how to make your diet healthier. The doctor will probably also tell you to get plenty of exercise. Both diet and exercise are important for maintaining a healthy weight.

FOOD SMARTS QUICK QUIZ

Here's your chance to prove that you've been paying attention to our monthly newsletters. Read the following statements. Then decide whether each one is true or false.

1. Brown eggs are more nutritious than white eggs.

2. Sweet potatoes have more calories than white potatoes.

3. Romaine lettuce has more vitamin C than iceberg lettuce.

4. Most people eat more salt in their diets than they need.

5. If people want to eat healthy diets, they should never eat at fast food restaurants.

6. Low-fat milk has less fat than skim milk.

7. Whole wheat bread is more nutritious than white bread.

Answers

1. False. Brown and white eggs have the same nutritional value.
2. False. Both sweet and white potatoes have about 1 calorie per gram.
3. True. Romaine lettuce has about ten times the vitamin C of iceberg lettuce.
4. True. People only need about 5 milliliters (1 teaspoon) of salt each day.
5. False. An occasional meal at your favorite fast food joint is not a bad thing.
6. False. Skim milk contains less fat than low-fat milk and about half the fat of whole milk.
7. True. White bread is made with flour that has had the *bran*, or brown outer layer, removed from the grain. This outer layer contains important nutrients.

GLOSSARY

Additive A substance added to a food to preserve it or to increase its effectiveness.

Adipose cell A body cell that stores fat.

Artificial sweetener A manufactured chemical used to sweeten food.

Ascorbic acid Vitamin C.

Calcium A metallic element necessary for building strong bones.

Calorie A unit of heat; a measure of the energy in food.

Carbohydrates A group of nutrients that provide energy; sugars and starches.

Chemistry The branch of science that deals with the composition, structure, and properties of matter.

Cholesterol A waxy substance found in human tissues.

Contagious Transmitted by contact or by some other means.

Deficiency Lack of an adequate amount.

Diabetes A disease in which the body cannot process sugar efficiently.

Digestion The process by which food is broken down into a form the body can use.

Enzyme A protein molecule that speeds up chemical reactions but is not changed itself.

Fats A group of nutrients that provide energy and building blocks for development of some body systems.

Fructose A sugar found naturally in fruits.

Glucose A sugar found in fruits and vegetables; the sugar metabolized in your cells.

Ingredient One material that goes into a mixture.

Insulin A protein hormone that enables the body to use sugar and other carbohydrates by regulating sugar metabolism.

Lactose A sugar found in milk.

Metabolism The process of breaking down food to yield energy to keep an organism alive and functioning.

Minerals Substances that work with vitamins, necessary for growth and development. Minerals come from soil. People get them by eating plants or by eating animals that eat plants.

Molecule The smallest part of a substance that is made up of two or more atoms.

Nutrient A chemical found in food that helps keep an organism alive and active.

Nutrition The science or study of proper balanced diets to promote health, especially in humans.

Nutritionist A person who studies foods and diets.

Obesity The condition of having an excess amount of body fat.

Plaque A sticky film composed of bacteria, food, and saliva that forms on your teeth; also fatty deposits in the arteries that may lead to a heart attack.

Proteins A group of nutrients that provide energy and building blocks for growth and repair of body tissues; found in meats and vegetables.

Rickets A disease in which the bones become soft and deformed due to a lack of vitamin D.

Salivary gland A gland that empties its secretions into the mouth to start the process of digestion.

Scurvy A disease caused by a lack of vitamin C and characterized by loosening of the teeth, softening of the gums, and bleeding under the skin.

Sickle-cell anemia A disease in which the red blood cells become sickle-shaped instead of round.

Sodium A soft, silvery, metallic element necessary for human nutrition. Table salt contains sodium.

Stroke A sudden weakening, loss of consciousness, or loss of the power to move or feel caused by the blockage of blood vessels in the brain.

Sucrose A sugar found in sugar beets and sugar cane.

Supplement A source of vitamins or minerals that is taken in addition to food.

Viral Caused by a virus.

Viruses A large group of disease-producing agents smaller than bacteria and dependent on living cells for reproduction and growth.

Vitamins Nutrients needed in small quantities that are essential for good health.

ANSWER FOR PAGE 29 *Peanut butter*